Simply
Watercolours

igloobooks
.com

Published in 2012
Igloo Books Ltd
Cottage Farm
Sywell
NN6 0BJ

www.igloobooks.com

© Copyright 2012 Igloo Books Ltd

FIR003 0712
10 9 8 7 6 5 4 3 2 1
ISBN 978-0-85780-735-9

Printed in and manufactured in China

Contents

Introduction

Learning to paint is exciting, creative and above all great fun. It opens up new possibilities in discovering the world that surrounds you. Painting will teach you to become more observant and help you to express yourself through the medium of colour and composition.

Everyone, at some point in their life, has probably sat down and painted a picture. More often than not this would have been as a child; when we are at school we are given the opportunity to express ourselves through art. Sadly though, for a lot of people this activity is lost or forgotten once formal education is over. For others, art never leaves them, whilst some re-discover their enthusiasm for painting later on in life.

This book will help any budding artist to become more informed and experienced, as painting is an ongoing process of learning and discovery. The easy-to-follow exercises will teach you the skills required to compose and paint pictures of your own choosing. The basic rules of composition and perspective will be demonstrated and diverse subjects such as landscapes and portraits will be explored.

The key factor in the process of painting is to master the basic techniques used in watercolour.

The importance of how to use a sketchbook to record ideas for pictures and the practical use as a learning tool will also be illustrated. Throughout the book the exercises will help you to build up the skills and confidence, to allow you to start creating beautiful pictures with your own unique style. There will be lots of tips on

mastering simple techniques, which, with practice, will give you an excellent basis for producing your paintings. Above all, painting is about having fun with art and using the skills you have learnt from this book.

- The content in this book will provide you with examples of step-by-step methods and techniques which will help you to achieve the necessary skills to develop confidence and technical ability.

- Learn about the usefulness of practicing techniques in a sketchbook and gathering reference material to start creating unique compositions.

- When creating a composition, learn the importance of careful planning with a simple check list.

- Create the illusion of a three dimensional space within a painting by mastering perspective and accurate proportion.

- Discover the different range of painting equipment available and how to choose the best for your needs.

Painting Defined

The processes of learning to paint may seem a daunting prospect as there are so many different areas to think about, from understanding colour to which type of paint to use, but everyone has the potential to be able to paint.

Throughout history, painting has been one of the most fundamental activities that human beings have done. To record the hunt as in the prehistoric cave paintings, through to the ancient civilisations of the Egyptians and the Greeks.

Many painters have documented the times that they live in and the events in their history, as well as the important subjects, such as their kings and queens. From the formal portraits and countless battles, to simple scenes of everyday life as in the paintings of Van Gogh, painting is part of our lives and history. Painting can also make bold statements and has been seen at times to be politically subversive, as in the Surrealists and Cubists movements.

Throughout history painting has had the power to create emotional responses and you can be part of that process and part of that history.

Many people find painting pictures a challenge because they feel that they have to produce a life like representation of the subject they are looking at. In some

cases, they create their own pressure by believing that they have to produce that 'masterpiece' with as much detail in as possible.

Most often, a good painting is about what you leave out rather than what you put in, so the work on the painting can be minimal and yet still convey some kind of message or emotion.

A good artist over time will learn what to leave out of a painting and what to put in, often by trial and error, to create a visually stimulating piece of work. As there are no strict rules in painting, there is nothing to prevent an artist from rendering a scene in any way that they feel will benefit the overall composition. This book will assist you in interpreting any subject in a

fresh and spontaneous method, which will give emotion and purpose to your paintings.

A painting should be comprised of a series of marks that bring feeling and often meaning. A good painting will work on that level, as opposed to a composition that lacks depth and has little understanding of the overall subject.

A painting of a subject is basically an interpretation as the artist views it and every artist will, with practice, begin to develop an individual style of their own.

Before you begin there are certain criteria to consider. If you decide to create an objective painting, you will be looking to produce a realistic or 'lifelike' representation in your composition.

This will give an accurate and factual look to the picture and many illustrators use this method to create works of art. A subjective painting will be far more expressive and have passion and emotion, which at times may result in a very abstract composition. Many good artists manage to find a balance between the two styles of painting.

The effect that you wish to create will be determined by what the painting material will let you produce. For instance, watercolour will give you thin washes of colour, which can be blended together. By the end of this book, you will have a clear understanding of how the various paints perform and what is available to you. You will also have knowledge on the best methods for use on your paintings. You will be guided through the basic rules of using contrasting or complimentary colours within your compositions to create interesting effects.

If you feel inspired by a subject such as a beautiful flower or a stunning view, then you are halfway to creating a successful painting. Most of your paintings will work if you connect with the subject and

really start to understand what you are looking at. It is worth trying out the same subject from different perspectives and other styles to prevent your work from becoming predictable or stale.

Think 'out of the box' and try a change from time to time, which should give you a fresh perspective on your favourite subject. Trying new things can be daunting if you let them and working within your comfort zone is easy, but challenging yourself as an artist is exciting. You may discover that you have talents you never thought possible. There is no right or wrong way to paint, there are no rules and no one to tell you that you can't do that, there are only techniques and methods of application.

It is up to the individual artist to experiment and gain more knowledge of the materials and subject matter, which in time will give more confidence to creating stunning works of art. No one artist starts out brilliant at painting, it comes with practice.

Plan and Prepare

Before embarking on a painting, you should have a mental checklist of what is required for producing a piece of art. If carefully planned, a painting is more likely to work successfully.

Consider these points when planning a painting:

- What expression or emotion do you want your painting to say? Which style of painting do you want, objective or subjective?

- Will you be working from photographs or memory, or are you going to work on location? Will you be using a sketchbook to record all the relevant information? You may need to make a series of sketches, some subjective to capture a mood or feeling, or more objective studies to ensure you have all the relevant information required for your paintings.

- Are you working in a 'landscape' or 'portrait' format? What viewpoint will you approach?

The more experience you have, the more confident you will become and these sort of considerations will become second nature to you. If you make some mistakes, you can learn from them maybe even achieve some fantastic results from experimenting.

Creating compositions

Composition is the design and layout within the space of the painting. It should be influenced by the elements that are included in the image or what you want your picture to say. This can include mood, atmosphere, impact, as well as the actual subject matter.

An important factor within

a composition is the use of space. Every object and space within the design, have a direct relation to each other. These are called the positive and negative spaces, the positive being the subject and the negative being the space around and between the subject. For example, in a landscape the positive space would be the subjects such as trees, hills, buildings and so on. The negative space would be the areas around and between the objects.

If these elements are interwoven together successfully then the composition and the overall image will work well and be successful. Applying contrasts within a composition will also enhance it.

For example, to show how dominant something is, position a small object next to it. Other examples of this are, place light next to dark, thick next to thin, shadow next to light, these contrasts will enliven and improve any composition.

Balance in a composition is important, as you don't want the picture to appear much heavier on one side than the other.

- Add an element within the whole composition to act as the main focal point of interest. Try not to place it too centrally in the design as the eye will naturally go direct to that point. Alternatively,

try to lead the eye around the painting by making the composition as interesting as you can.

- Placing objects in rows could make your picture appear boring and lifeless. By varying the perspective, you will create more movement around the picture and also gain a greater depth in the image.

The Golden Mean

It is best to avoid placing your main subject, or objects too close to the centre of the composition, or to split the picture centrally, either vertically or horizontally. If this is done your eye will be lead directly to the midpoint in

the picture and the rest of the composition will be lost.

When using a rectangular format either horizontally or vertically, the traditional rule to apply is the Golden Mean and also known as the Golden Rectangle or Golden Ratio. This is a principle first devised by the Renaissance painters, who believed it was the perfect layout. It is a format for dividing up a rectangle using geometry, so this principle will help you in designing and structuring your composition.

The Golden Mean is based on the mathematical relationship between three points on a straight line, a simple way to explain it would be that a picture should be divided up by a ratio of 2:3. So any important aspect or element within the composition should be placed about two thirds of the way across the paper. This will help to create a pleasing and harmonious picture. You can use this principle on both the vertical and the horizontal lines, so it is ideal for landscape and portrait viewpoints.

Portable Viewfinder

For ease, you can make a portable viewfinder or use the digital display on your camera. This is a very practical tool that can be easily made from a fairly thick piece of card about 10cm x 14cm (4" x 5.5"). Cut out a rectangle from the centre of the sheet. To use the viewfinder, hold it away from you, shutting one eye, whilst looking through the hole at the composition. This will assist you to 'frame' your subject to decide the best viewpoint in which to begin drawing.

Perspective, the basics

Perspective is an element in drawing that helps to give a sense of depth and realism. If you look up along a straight road, the outer edges of the road seem to converge as they fade into the distance.

Where to two edges meet in the distance, this is called the vanishing point.

In fact we know these lines are parallel and do not converge, but the optical illusion created gives us the sense of distance. The effect of perspective is relatively easy to produce. Obviously, the more you practice drawing perspective the easier it will become.

Perspective's main elements
Horizon LineThe horizon line is the distant horizontal line which should be roughly level with the observer's eye. The line will change position as the observer changes also, for example if you look at the line from a sitting position and then change to a standing position.

- Aerial perspective is different to the other two types in that the vanishing point can be above or below the horizon line. When used along side oblique perspective, the two types will give the subject in a composition an illusion of height or depth.

Parallel perspective exercises.
As there is only one vanishing point in parallel perspective, start with this one first to get an understanding how perspective works. Refer to the box in the illustration as a guide. Notice all the parallel lines converging to a single point.

- Draw a similar box several times and try changing its width and height.

- Having done that, attempt the two illustrations of the room using the same principle as the box. See how all the vertical and horizontal lines are parallel to the edge of the paper, the same as the box. Only the parallel lines that recede are affected. A little later try also moving the vanishing point along the horizon line.

View point
The direction of where the observer is looking will determine the viewpoint.

Vanishing Points
Drawings with perspective will have at least one vanishing point, usually on the horizon line. There are three vanishing point perspectives, Parallel, Oblique and Aerial perspective. These three types are related to the number of vanishing points within a composition.

- Parallel perspective is when all the parallel lines converge to one point.

- Oblique perspective is where there are two vanishing points on the horizon line. This perspective creates two sets of converging lines which meet at their respective vanishing points.

Oblique perspective exercises

When using oblique perspective, you can draw subjects that are placed at an angle. This is most useful when painting buildings, as most often they are at different angles to each other.

- Place two vanishing points on the horizon line. Draw your guide lines from these points to create the lines which converge at the front edge of the box. Try, distant, close-up, high and low view exercises.

- If the box is in the distance, it will appear a lot smaller with less sloping of the sides, as opposed to a box that is much closer.

- When the vanishing points are close to the subject on a normal horizon line, the object will appear very close.

- A low viewpoint is when the horizon line moves down

the box. This makes the converging lines above the horizon appear steeper.

- If the horizon line is moved up above the subject, this will create a high viewpoint looking down on the subject.

- When a third or 'aerial'

vanishing point is added, a sense of height is given to a composition.

Further ways of creating perspective

Tone and colour will also create a sense of perspective and will be explained later in the book.

Colour Palette

Without the proper use of colour, the perfect composition, use of tones and the right mediums will all be made redundant. Studying this useful guide on colour will assist you in making the most out of your palette.

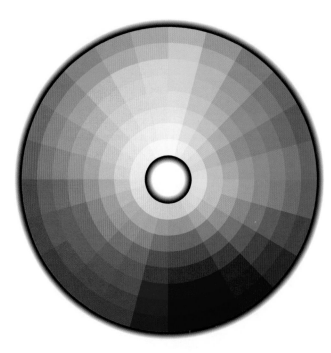

The Colour Wheel

The colour wheel is a visual illustration of the three main qualities that make up any colour. These are hue, tonal value and intensity.

- A hue is the name of a colour such as red, orange, violet, all are common examples.

- Tonal value is the lightness or darkness of a colour. To darken or shade a hue, add black pigment and to lighten or tint a hue add white pigment.

- Intensity is how bright or dull a hue is. The more brilliant and vivid a colour is the stronger the intensity. For example

yellow has a strong intensity, whereas violet has a dull appearance due to its weaker intensity.

- The colour wheel is made up of three types of hue, primary, secondary and tertiary.

- Paint a colour wheel in your sketchbook to help you understand more about using colour. Draw a circle and divide it into six equal segments.

Primary colours

There are three primary colours, red, yellow and blue. These colours cannot be mixed from any other colours and are pure and very bright. They are easily recognised whereas other colours or subtle hues are not so easy to distinguish. Paint the colour wheel with the three primary colours and positioning the yellow at the top, as indicated.

Secondary colours

When you mix yellow and red together, you make orange which is known as a secondary colour. Secondary colours are always made from mixing two primary colours. Add yellow and blue to make green and red to blue to make violet. Include these colours to your colour wheel as indicated.

Complementary colours

All primary colours are complemented by a secondary colour, never another primary, for instance red and green are complementary colours. On the colour wheel, these colours are directly opposite and are visually opposed to each other. Study and use the colour wheel to learn about which colours complement each other.

When using complementary colours within a composition, use them sparingly as they will stand out and could appear too jarring to the eye.

Tertiary colours
Tertiary colours are made up of a primary colour mixed with a secondary colour. For instance, yellow – green, red – orange and blue – violet.

These are all examples of tertiary colours and placed on the colour wheel between each related primary and secondary colour.

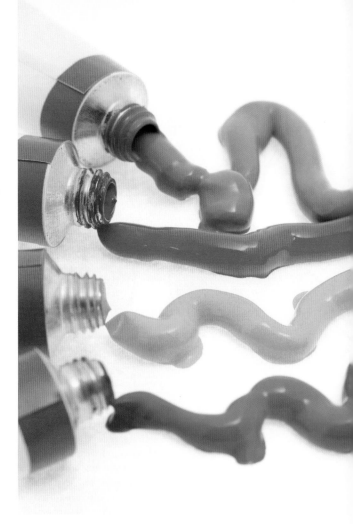

Colour mixing with black
Mising colours with black will give them the appearance of being shaded. They will look duller and darker in colour.

Colour mixing with white
Mixing colour with white will give the appearance of a softer and much lighter colour.

Colour to Create Mood

Good use of colour can convey a sense of mood within a composition and initiate an emotive response from the viewer.

If you look at the two photographs, both are of still scenes, but the mood in each of them, because of the colour is quite different.

The picture of the boat is predominantly blue in colour and is a tonal value composition. Because of the colours, it is cool, serene and almost unnerving in its calmness, which also gives a sense of emptiness. This is reflected beautifully in the empty boat, which appears to be abandoned.

The photograph of the sunset edging over the pyramids is a scene of solitude and yet it still appears warm and inviting. The golden yellow tones radiating across the sky and the shadows in the sand have warmed up the whole scene.

These examples show how important the correct use of colour can be when creating a composition.

Use the colour wheel to help you select the appropriate colours to convey the moods you wish to produce.

Materials

For the very best results, it is essential to have the right equipment. This practical guide will assist you in understanding the tools and materials available to you.

Paints

Watercolour paints are coloured pigments mixed with Gum Arabic and Glycerine. Once dry, watercolour paints can sometimes appear insipid and pale, but when mastered you can create beautiful spontaneous paintings.

- Watercolour paint comes in two forms, in tubes and pans. Tube paint is a thick concentrated liquid which is squeezed out and thinned with water.

- As tubes are rich in pigment, these are best suited for work that requires a higher concentration of colour.

- Pans are semi-dry blocks of paint that are usually supplied in a box. If painting outside, take a box of pan watercolour paints with you. They are easy to transport, fairly inexpensive and have a huge range of colours.

Brushes

Good brushes are very important in painting pictures, so only buy quality ones. Cheap brushes do not perform well and last only a fraction of the time of the good ones.

There are many sizes available but a beginner will only require three or four brushes, small (size No.1), medium (size No. 6) and large (size No. 14). Perhaps a flat brush could be added to the list at a later date, for larger washes of colour.

There are several types of brushes available for watercolour painting:

- Brushes made from real hair, but there are some excellent synthetic brushes as well.

- Round brushes are shaped to a fine point which allows for detail work when the tip is applied to the paper surface. They can also be used to apply a wash, depending on the size of the brush, when swept sideways across the painting surface. With this

technique you can apply large amounts of colour as you go.

- Flat chisel-shaped brushes are best suited for laying washes over larger areas. The flat brushes with rounded ends are known as 'Filberts' and fan brushes are also very useful, especially when painting grasses.

- Always wash out your brushes thoroughly when you have finished painting. Shape them back to a point and dry them with the bristles pointing upwards. Never leave them in the water pot facing down or stored in the same manner, as this will damage the point on the brush so will not work as efficiently in the future.

Painting equipment

For mixing your watercolours you will need a palette. Boxes with pan colours usually have a palette provided, or you can buy a palette separately from most art retailers. Alternatively, another option is a clean white plate, which can be used and then washed afterwards.

Water pots with screw-top lids are a must if you are painting outside. You will need two; one for washing your brushes and the other for clean water to mix with your paints.

A sketching pencil and a putty rubber are essential tools for drawing your initial guidelines prior to painting. These are explained in more detail later on.

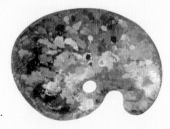

Papers

- Watercolour papers come in many different types and are available in pads, books and as single sheets. They are graded according to weight (gsm, or grams per metre squared), which determines the thickness and they are usually rough in texture which allows the watercolour to key to the paper.

- An absorbent paper will soak up the pigment, whereas a shiny paper will not accept the paint readily. Good quality cartridge paper is ideal for watercolour sketching, but do not get it too wet, as it will buckle with excessive water. Proper watercolour paper is the best for most paintings.

- Hot-pressed paper is a smooth surfaced paper, whereas rough paper is heavily textured.

Cold-pressed papers are a mixture of the two and are most commonly used. Textured papers are essential for watercolour painting, as the paint requires a pitted surface in which the pigment can sit. There are various grades of textured paper that will give very different results.

- 300gsm paper is good for most painting mediums including pencil washes, watercolour and also pen and ink.

Canvas

The traditional surface for oil painting is canvas, but it can also be used in watercolour painting. Stretched canvas or canvas boards are available in many sizes and varieties. Hardboard or medium density fibre board (mdf), coated in at least two coats of gesso or white emulsion are good surface alternatives.

Storing your materials

A plastic toolbox from a DIY store is an excellent storage solution for your art materials. It is light, robust easy to clean and has a carrying handle.

A good art folder is another essential piece of kit, as it can store your loose papers and drawings. They come in a number of varieties and prices, so check them out at your local art supplier.

Papers

There are many different papers for the artist to choose from and come in many forms. They are available in book form such as sketch pads and individual sheets. Paper is graded by its weight (gsm, or grams per metre squared), which determines the thickness of the paper. It is available in a huge range of colours and textures.

Some papers are textured

to produce certain effects when painted on and some suit certain materials. Other papers are more universal and used with a wide variety of different materials. It is worth experimenting with different papers to see what can be achieved and suits your needs.

- The smoother papers are good for pencil sketches

and detailed compositions created in pen and ink where the lines appear clean and fine. Cartridge paper is the good all rounder of papers and is often used in many sketchbooks as the ideal paper for this purpose. Very smooth papers are the hot-pressed papers, which give a hard, unforgiving line whereas the cold-pressed papers are a little more textured producing softer lines.

- Textured paper is the ideal paper for watercolours as it well suited to produce different effects from the various grades. There are some very coarse grades and others not so much, which give soft, rich tones.

Things to look for in the weight of paper:

- 150gsm is good for drawing and sketching.
- 180gsm being heavier in weight is more suited for soft pencil and charcoal drawings.
- 300gsm is ideal for watercolour pencil work, line and wash and for general mixed media compositions.

Graphite pencils

Pencils come in varying degrees of hardness from 9H to 8B. Pencils are incredibly versatile and the most commonly material used for sketching and drawing.

- When grading pencils, H indicates 'hard'. H pencils are best suited for technical drawings due to the hard grey marks that they make. They can indent the paper and are often difficult to erase.

- B pencils are 'soft' pencils and are the most widely used pencils for drawing by artists. They produce darker, softer marks and are easily removed with an eraser. These types of pencils are also easier to manipulate, blend and smudge.

- A good set of pencils will include a 2H pencil for detail drawing, an HB for basic work and note taking, a 2B for drawing and sketching and a 4B and a 6B for darker tones and heavier shading.

Other types of drawing material to consider are graphite sticks which are made of pure graphite and used in the same manner as pencils.

- Wider strokes and marks can be achieved when used on an angle.

- Sepia sketching pencils are a brown pigmented pencil, traditionally used for sketching a subject on to a canvas. Used on paper it produces a pale brown line, which is easily smudged and water soluble.

- Sanguine sketching pencils are richer brown pencils and are also used for drawing on to a canvas. Often these pencils are used on coloured paper with white chalk as highlights.

Watercolour pencils

Watercolour pencils are a mixture of pigment and clay and all sorts of effects can be created with these soluble pencils. The pencils at first are applied in the normal manner and then water is added with a brush to create a watercolour wash effect. Dry pencil work can be added on top once the water has dried to create various textures and tones. Use them in a watercolour composition to produce a mixed media painting.

Basic equipment

These are the very basic items you should have regardless of the style of painting you are working on. Use these items with any of the suggested materials from the previous sections in the book.

- Pencils, 2H, HB, 2B, 4B and 6B.
- A putty rubber and harder eraser.
- A spiral-bound sketchpad and a bound sketchbook.
- A craft knife and pencil sharpener.
- Paper tissues or soft rags for wiping off paint and cleaning.
- A roll of masking tape for securing work to the drawing board.
- A wooden or metal easel if required.

Learning to See

As a beginner you should spend a lot of time drawing, observing and really looking at a variety of different subjects.

Learning to see is a skill like any other and this is something that every artist has to practice and master.

- Practice looking at how things relate to each other to help you compose good paintings. Observe the way shapes relate to one another and do they overlap? How are they grouped together and where is your eye naturally drawn to? Could this be made into an interesting composition? Once again look at the same subjects, but think about tone, texture and colour.

- Experiment with your subjects in two different ways, objective and then subjective as previously mentioned in the book.

- Take into account that all objects, spaces and subjects can change according to various factors such as time, light, mood, etc. The subject may dictate the medium or style of painting, or drawing you wish to produce.

Think of the practicalities for instance, if you are sketching skies or a busy market place on holiday.

Pencils, pens or watercolours would be ideal to capture the essence of the subjects and are very portable.

- Think about your objectives and what the composition is about.

- Is it going to be a sketch, research material or a finished composition?

- Will it be objective or subjective and how can you communicate your perception of the subject? Take into account the previous exercises and how you can relate them to your aims for a particular picture.

- Attempt all manner of different subjects as the more you draw and the broader your subject knowledge, the quicker you will begin to develop your own style. Understanding many subjects will assist your imagination to inventing your own compositions, but you do need to have a basic technical knowledge to turn imagination into art.

- Develop your hand-to-eye coordination and remember to allow your own interpretation of the subject to help shape your composition.

With enthusiasm, even though you would be thinking of the technical aspects of the work, you should be halfway there in creating a visually stimulating composition.

Sketchbook

Sketching a few minutes each day will improve your eye-to hand coordination, allowing you to attempt ever-increasing challenges in techniques and compositions.

The best way to progress as an artist is to keep a sketchbook that you can practise in every day.

The Sketchbook

The sketchbook is basically an artist's aid and is an essential piece of equipment. It can hold all the information that you would need in the form of drawings that you produce, notes and details of various subjects within it and cuttings for reference.

When buying a sketchbook consider how big it is. Too big a sketchbook will not transport so easily and can be quite awkward to work with on a location. However, it should be big enough to hold all the information you wish to gather comfortably. A consideration is to have two books, one small sketchbook for your pocket or handbag and a larger one for home studies.

Your sketchbooks should be made of cartridge paper in a spiral-bound pad or hardback books. However, if you prefer to work directly watercolour at this stage, then you may wish to purchase one that suits this.

How to use your sketchbook

Your sketchbook should not be a finished composition, but a personal visual and technical aid. It is for your development and confidence without fear of judgement, as you can make as many mistakes in it as you wish. Practise some sketches without the use of a rubber and that way you can see any mistakes you have made. You can refer back to them later when you draw that subject again.

- Practise new techniques in your sketchbook to hone your skills, everything from small individual studies to lines and textures.

- Also within your sketchbook, try working out and practising the rules of perspective or attempt new subjects. Try different mediums and techniques or even invent new ways to mix certain mediums together. Some will work, while others will not but you will learn a lot from trying.

- One of the crucial sketchbook functions is to act as a reference point for more finished compositions. Record such details as tone, texture and colour with any other information that will have an influence on the final composition. View and draw your subjects from different angles to help you visualise them more clearly, in finalising the structure of your pictures.

Sketchbook exercises

- Choose a subject such as a fruit or a view from a window and draw it at least four times or more, over a period of a week. The more times you draw the subject, the more you begin to understand it. You will see how your interpretation changes on the later attempts and you should find your sketches becoming more fluid.

- You can try limiting yourself to a time scale in which to produce a quick sketch of a simple subject. Start at two minutes each sketch and then decrease the time until you reach a time of 30 seconds per sketch. This will speed up your sketching ability and will make you concentrate on just drawing the essence of the subject. Don't worry too much about drawing detail at this stage.

- A good exercise for your sketchbook is in knowing what to paste into it as reference. Don't get too

carried away as the book will become too bulky, but do paste cuttings from magazines, photographs, bits of fabric, even dried leaves. So long as these items are useful as reference for later paintings, or spark an idea for a composition.

- Try a limited use of colour, what's known as 'limited palette'. Use maybe only three or four colours in a composition or when colouring a sketch.

- Experiment with different drawing or writing tools to explore what types of marks these will make. Some interesting ideas and drawing techniques can be achieved by using items such as ballpoint pens.

- If your subject has lots of exciting qualities for example, good texture or tone, form or colour, then make several sketches of each in turn.

- Create an abstract interpretation of an everyday object to be able to break it down to its simplest form. This will help you in capturing the essence of a subject.

- Repeat these exercises over and over again with different subjects, materials and colours. Try to do at least two or more a week to keep you artistically 'fit'.

Sketchbooks on field trips

An important function of your sketchbook is to be a portable studio. Many artists find inspiration when they are out on field trips and amongst nature and also everyday scenes. Keep a sketchbook to hand at all times whilst out as a subject will grab your attention when you least expect it, or you can pre-plan a field trip to gather reference material. If you are planning a reference-gathering trip, you should make some basic preparations to ensure the whole trip is worthwhile.

Planning field trips

Here are a few basic steps to consider when organising a field trip.

- Be prepared for the weather, in some places it can be unpredictable, but this is what adds drama and makes good pictures. However, take a foldable raincoat if it is likely to pour down and some refreshments. Dress appropriately, as you will not feel like sketching if you are too hot or too cold.

- Carry your art materials in a sturdy bag, such as a rucksack, as you may have to travel quite a distance to reach a certain location to sketch.

- A quality waterproof bag will last for years and protect all your equipment.

- Carry a diverse range of sketching materials, to capture different aspects of a subject. Remember to also take a bottle of water for your watercolours and water-soluble pencils.

- You will need a craft knife to sharpen your pencils, a rubber and a clean rag, a selection of brushes and paper clips to stop your paper blowing in the wind.

- Some artists take a small collapsible stool to sit on, but a plastic ground sheet will suffice as it is easily transported and fairly light.

- When you are working in the open landscape, you will find that you are not

in control of the subject or the surroundings. Also the light will be constantly changing, which will affect the shadows. This means you will have to work faster than you would in your home and learn to sketch quickly.

- Don't waste a lot of time on detail or elements you can add later and make a few notes to accompany your drawings to help you later on.

- Focus only on the essential information of the subject and choose the materials that will help you to achieve that goal.

Photographs and notes

You can support your sketches with photographs or notes. If your sketches are drawn in pencil or charcoal, you can use the photographs to provide colour information or the notes to describe the quality of the light, which sometimes photos cannot capture.

- Use your photographs to give you different compositional viewpoints.

- When photographing your subject, capture specific

elements such as colour, form and close-ups of textures for reference later.

- Subjects such as birds flying are difficult to sketch, but easier to capture with the use of a camera.

- Photographs should be a starting point for most compositions and not relied on as the only source of reference.

Simple notes or bullet points

will help you to cross-reference your drawings and photographs much more easily.

Field Studies
- Sketch a view from different viewpoints and with different mediums, over a period of several visits.

- For wildlife field studies, try very quick sketches to create a more fluid representation, containing the basic elements of the subject.

Concentrate on the overall proportions and posture and don't get too bogged down with details at this stage. If you are sketching animals or people, they have a habit of moving around. The best way to approach this is to keep drawing the subjects in different positions then you can rework them as they return to each of those positions.

- For flowers or trees, try sketching them over a period of a few weeks to see how they change.

- When choosing a theme such as trees or buildings, gather as much material as possible in the form of sketches, photographs and magazine clippings.

- Always have your sketchbook handy when you are on holiday. Different places can provide new subjects for you to tackle with a vast array of stunning landscapes, wildlife, buildings and people.

- Sketch a scene at different times of the day to see how the shadows fall and the tonal values change. The early morning light quality will be totally different to that at dusk.

- Sketching from life will give your compositions a firm foundation of form and structure. Knowing how a subject moves or grows, changes according to light or weather conditions, will help you to interpret your subject with far more clarity.

The following chapters contain exercises for you to practice in your sketchbook. These will be a continuous record of your progress as an artist.

Artistic Marks

You must learn some basic drawing skills before you start to paint, as you will need to support your paintings with research sketches, as well as drawing guidelines of your subjects on your paper or canvas.

Basic drawing techniques

When holding a pencil most people grip it near the drawing point then move their fingers and wrist. This produces a tight linear control much the same as writing.

For the more artistic way, hold the pencil lightly, releasing the tension from your fingers and wrist.

The drawing action should now come from your shoulder and through your elbow, with the wrist absorbing some of the action but still remaining loose. Holding the shaft of the pencil further up will affect the marks that you choose to make. The higher up the pencil your fingers are the more fluid and loose the line. Avoid resting your hand on the paper if you can whilst drawing.

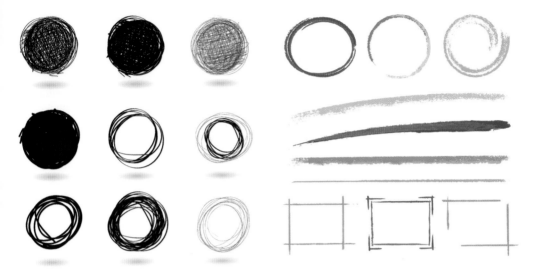

Exercise 1

With a HB pencil, hold it as though you were going to start writing. Now draw looped, wavy and zigzag lines. You will find that it feels rather restrictive drawing with a tense hand and wrist.

Exercise 2

Use the same pencil, but this time move your fingers up the shaft and repeat the exercise. You should find this action a little more fluid.

Exercise 3

Once again repeat the exercise, but hold the pencil shaft even further up. The lines will now look very free and spontaneous. By comparing all three exercises, you will see the difference of how changing your hand position on the pencil will affect the marks that you make.

Exercise 4

In drawing it may seem as though there are unlimited types of lines and marks to make, but in fact there are four basic styles of line to use.

The four types of lines are:

- Wire line, a clean and constant line which you would use for sharp definite outlines.
- Calligraphic line, as an uneven and variable width line, it is useful for emphasising tonal qualities.
- Broken line, this being a short line used repeatedly to convey a more subtle outline.
- Repeated line is a free flowing, fluid style of line.

Basic watercolour techniques

Watercolour paint is a delicate medium so fluid and gentle strokes are required. Use flowing strokes with the brush and keep your grip relaxed.

Use the tip only for detail and three quarters of the brush pressed to the paper for wider strokes.

Use a No.6 brush for the following exercises.

- Paint a line with the tip of the brush.
- Apply more pressure to create a thicker line.
- Wipe excess paint off the brush to make an uneven and broken 'Dry Brush' line.
- Try using a slightly thicker paint and the tip of the brush once again.
- Practice a curved line with a more fluid paint mixture.
- Draw with the brush, try the three-sided box and fill in with colour.
- Experiment with a range of different marks and try various water and paint mixes.

Flat tone wash

A fundamental element of watercolour painting is the 'wash' technique. For this technique, use a cold-pressed watercolour paper. Use a large (No.6 or higher), soft watercolour brush.

- Mix a small amount of paint with plenty of water in a palette and enough to cover the area. Watercolours tend to dry paler, so allow for this when mixing.

- Load the brush with the watercolour mix and using a long, broad stroke, paint an even band of colour straight across the top of the paper.

You will notice that the paint will collect and pool at the bottom edge.

- Reload your brush again and repeat the process but this time, pick up the excess at the bottom with the second brushstroke as you go.

- If you stop halfway the wash will dry and look uneven, so keep working until you have finished.

- Apply wet paint onto wet paper, or into painted areas that are still wet to produce a wet-in-wet technique. This creates a soft blurring effect, which is excellent for painting dramatic skies.

- Paint a graduated wash, in a similar fashion to the flat wash by adding more water to the paint, thinning each stroke down.

- Layer different colour washes together to give a translucent and almost ethereal effect when the colours blend and combine together.

- You can soften edges of painted areas by lifting off some colour with a wet brush. Use a soft tissue to remove pigment and excess paint to create a translucent effect.

Using the Colour Palette

Warm and Cool colours

If you were to draw a line through the colour wheel, from the yellow down to the violet, you would separate the two halves into warm and cool colour palettes.

The warm colours would be the reds and oranges, think of sunsets, fire or the sun. Whereas the cool colours would be the blues and greens, think of the sea or ice for blues and lush cool foliage for the greens.

A mixture of both warm and cool colours can be used in a composition; however, some striking effects can be achieved by using just warm or cool colours. The abstract paintings illustrated were each produced with colours from one side of the colour wheel. To show how a subject can appear different according to the colours chosen, the pears were painted in warm and then again in cool colour palettes.

For a balanced composition, use a mixture of the two types of colour palettes. The photographs of the bowl of apples and bananas seem cold and lifeless in the composition when in purely tonal colours. The yellow image is lifelike and warm whereas, the predominantly violet and green images seem to be quite stark.

This is something to bear in mind when showing highlights or shadows.

For example, if you are painting a tree, you can add yellow highlights and blue shadows to accentuate form and structure. You can also convey a sense of depth by painting warm colours in the foreground and cooler colours in the background.

Light & Dark colours

Depending on the tonal values used, a painting can be seen as light or dark, just as it could be viewed as warm or cool.

Most paintings have specific areas of light and dark, which can warm and forward or cool and recessive. By adding white to lighten or black to darken a colour will have a cooling effect on the colour it is mixed with.

If you are going to add white to a colour, start off by mixing tiny amounts of colour to the white paint. This is much easier than trying to lighten an existing colour and it will save you lots of paint in the process. A thing to remember is that most white in a painting will be tinted by another hue.

Another way to lighten or darken a colour is to add a colour which is close to the colour you wish to change. This will change the hue without cooling it down.

The watercolour painting of the

bird in flight is a light painting not just because of the light paint, but because the white of the paper was allowed to show through the pigments and in effect lighten them. Now the painting has a translucent, delicate look to it. In contrast, the painting of the female figure has a dark background. However, the light that falls on the figure and that light and makes her the focal point of the piece.

Still Life

Working on a still life composition is the best way to progress from sketching to creating more adventurous pictures.

These types of paintings will benefit you in setting up compositions that you have total control over, from the positioning of the subject to the lighting conditions.

Composing your Still Life

As you begin to tackle more complex compositions, as opposed to drawing simple sketches, it is best to start off still life studies.

With this type of picture you have total control over your working conditions and you can take your time, without the concern that it will move or change dramatically. It is wise not to attempt anything too complicated at first, so set up a simple still life with two or three basic shapes and colours.

If your still life is positioned near a window for the light source, you should bear in mind that the light conditions will change. A better alternative is to use an angle poise lamp which is easy to control and can be directed at the subject. The still life will now receive the exact amount of light and shadow required. The shape of the subject will dictate whether your composition will be landscape or portrait format.

As an example, a tall vase of flowers is best done as portrait, whereas a selection of scattered fruit is best painted in a landscape format. The illustrated oil painting of flowers and fruit is a good example of this.

Decide on the style of painting you wish to produce. Will it be a subjective composition, by capturing the abstract qualities of the subject? Or will it be objective, with a more accurate view of the subject matter, which will be a representational picture. The watercolour painting of the peach and banana illustrates this well.

You should try to make your compositions as exciting as possible, so observe the objects well to arrange them into interesting positions. The six illustrations of simple still life studies are examples of how to arrange the subjects within a composition.

Shapes such as circles work best when there is a variation in size. When not in a straight line, the bottle, circle and box form a more interesting composition. In the final example, the objects are grouped together as this is a better way to compose a still life, rather than all the objects being spread out evenly. Try and use a variety of different forms, heights and sizes to add extra interest.

Drawing rounded objects

When creating a still life composition, you will discover that many of the objects you wish to draw contain circles or curves. The simplest way to draw any rounded object is to break it down into one of three basic shapes: cylinder, cone or sphere. You would then add the detail once you have drawn the basic form.

Take a look at the top of a glass, plate or bottle from straight on and you will see it appears to be flat. However, when you tilt it forwards, you will notice that it is rounded. This flattened circular shape is known as an ellipse.

Practice a simple ellipse by drawing a flattened circle. Use a 2B pencil very lightly so you have a smooth motion. Repeat the exercise several times and gradually flatten the circle a little each time.

This will help you to get the feel for differently shaped ellipses.

object looks distorted. With practice you will be able to draw the ellipses at the correct depth.

Axis lines
To help you draw rounded objects more easily, use the axis lines to get the correct angle of the ellipse. Getting the right angle is important especially if the object is tilted.

The upright line indicates the height (or length) axis and the horizontal line is the depth (or width) axis.

Once you have drawn the height and depth axis, you can then start to draw in the circle or ellipse.

Try to draw each quarter section as a mirror image to the next. When drawing objects such a glass or bowl, you will need two horizontal axis lines to create two ellipses, one for the top and one for the base. Even when the object is at an angle, the ellipses must be parallel to each other, or the object will look distorted.

Drawing circles may seem difficult, but if you keep your wrist relaxed and draw with your whole arm, you will get better the more you practice. Don't press too hard on the pencil, so any mistakes you make can easily be rectified with an eraser.

Now you can try drawing the three main shapes: cylinder, cone and sphere. For the shapes to appear three dimensional, practice varying the depth of the ellipses. If you are under-drawing or over-drawing the shape of the ellipse, you will notice that the

Objects as simple shapes

If you look at the illustrated still life, you will notice that the objects within it can be broken down into easy to draw simple shapes. Continue on from the cylinder, cone and sphere method, to breakdown more complex three-dimensional objects.

Practice breaking down objects into simple shapes, as they will be much easier to draw. Start adding detail once you have captured the basic shape of the object.

Draw fairly lightly with the pencil when sketching in the shapes, so any guidelines can easily be removed.

Always remember to draw a central axis line so you can arrange the ellipses along it. You should still do this even when the object is at an angle. Notice how an ellipse is shallower and rounder at eye level, than one that is above or below eye level. Remember this when looking at your shapes.

Light and Shade

An extremely important element of still life painting is the use of light and shade and the effects it creates among the chosen subjects. The illustrations clearly demonstrate how the light source can change the look and feel of a still life.

By placing the light source in front of the subjects, extreme contrasts of light and shade are possible. However, when the light source is positioned above the subjects, the composition creates quite a different effect. This is now far more exciting tonal composition which gives a feeling of solidity. This is a better way of lighting a group of objects. It now creates a sense of drama between the various shapes, especially through the intensity of shadows.

When you are drawing objects that are close together and some parts are obscured and you cannot see them, this does not mean that those parts are not there. Bear this in mind when positioning your objects close together in your composition. This will ensure the depth of the composition is not distorted.

Finalising a piece

Still life paintings can be created using any objects that excite you to paint them. An exciting painting can be produced from a wide variety of different subject matters. The composition does not have to be in a formal or stuffy format, but could be in a more fluid and relaxed fashion. The brush strokes might be free and vibrant even though the subject is observational. The use of light and colour can be subjective.

Do not feel that you have to

capture every detail in the subject, as some of the best compositions are successful when they are not over worked.

Learn to give your composition space and concentrate on the necessary elements that you wish to express emotion and meaning.

- **Step one** – Break down the objects in the still life into basic, simple shapes. If drawn lightly, the working-out pencil lines can be erased as the more detailed sketch is completed. Keep the shapes very light and simple to start with. This means that if required, the position of some objects can be changed without having to erase detailed drawings.

- **Step two** – Start blocking in the basic tonal elements of light and shade with a No.6 brush. As the medium is watercolour, it is important to remember to work from light tones first then to dark tones. This is known as light

to dark. Once a dark pigment is applied onto your painting, you cannot paint over it with a lighter colour. Keep your colours to a minimum, you could use cadmium yellow, cerulean blue, ultramarine, burnt umber and raw umber, violet and white. Overlap simple washes of colour to produce different tones.

- **Step three** – Finally, add detail to the painting by including a few darker areas, which you can pick out using a charcoal pencil. This will add depth and definition to your composition. You can leave much of the outer area un-worked to allow the main subject to be the focal point of the picture.

Landscapes

A certain amount of organisation is important when attempting a landscape painting.

When you are attempting a landscape painting on location, you will have to factor in environmental influences such as the weather and the changing light conditions.

- Make a note on the position of your light source, such as in most cases the sun, or the moon or streetlight if you are working at night.

- From this position the highlights and shadows can be worked out where they will form. When the light changes and it does outside, you will have a basic reference point to work from.

- For your composition, use the Golden Mean principle to divide the basic areas up. This will help to ensure that your main subject is noat positioned too centrally, which will later detract from the rest of the picture.

- Taking notes in your sketchbook will help you to remember certain details that you may need later. They will also ensure consistency throughout the composition.

The more a composition breaks the rules, the more effective it will be, so don't be afraid to experiment and think 'outside of the box'.

Background elements & Skies

Many artists base a lot of their landscape work on particular elements of this type of painting, such as skies, water, sunsets or mountains. These are all crucial background features in landscape composition.

You should have a go at painting a variety of skies and water effects, either separately or within the same piece. Be spontaneous as the best effects are those you least expect. When you are painting natural looking skies or water scenes, try not to over-work them. You can use the following examples to help you.

Sky techniques

- For portraying a calm summer sky, try a graduated watercolour wash.
- Use wet-in-wet washes to create a cloudy sky effect.
- In a predominantly white sky, you can paint small areas of colour to represent the gaps in the clouds.
- Dramatic sunsets can also be created using the watery

brush technique.
- Very convincing are often applied smoothly, perhaps with a few wispy clouds painted in by dragging white paint across the surface.

Water techniques

- By scumbling watercolour paint, you can create a sense of rough seawater.
- Pick out reflections by using dashes of colour and leaving the white of the paper to act as the reflected light on the tips of the waves.
- Blend lines of paint together to give the illusion of lapping water.
- Scumble, drag and splatter paint to create waves and spray.

Trees & Flowers

Most landscapes that you see will contain some kind of greenery even industrial areas usually have some kind of wild plants growing on them.

When painting trees or flowers, texture is vital because it helps to give the illusion of movement in leaves or delicate flowers. Texture is crucial when painting rough bark.

Buildings

The best technique for making this subject easier is to leave out any unnecessary elements and only include the important aspects of the buildings. This technique will give you a sense of the building without getting overtaken by technicalities.

- Street scenes give the sense of perspective and ensure that your eye travels up the street. The buildings should bustle with the interesting architectural elements.
- Stand-alone buildings painted in the foreground are very foreshortened; these highlight the building's importance and it's relation to other figures within the painting.
- The lack of detail and form in a picture convey an impression of structure without the need to overwork the composition.
- Finally, for other elements that may require a more linear approach, these can be interpreted in interesting and fun ways, such as the sketch of the fence post or the illustration of a car.

Animals

There are so many incredible and beautiful animals out there that it is no wonder so many people choose to sketch and paint them. Animals can often be hard to capture on paper, either because they move around a lot or sometimes due to their complicated anatomy.

You can practice drawing proportions from still images such as photographs, but always try to see your subject in its natural environment where possible. This will give you a greater understanding of how it moves and generally behaves.

Your quick sketches may not be anatomically correct at first, but the more you practice, the more you will be able to capture the spirit of the subject.

- Pictures do not have to have great detail to capture a moment in time, such as a leap of a cat or a bird in flight.
- The sketch of the cow with its calf could captured the gentle nature of the subject.
- When drawing and painting

animals, it is essential to sketch as much as possible in your sketchbook to act as reference material. Always try to capture and convey the animal's essence and spirit.

Portraits

Throughout history the human figure has been featured in paintings, including those on cave walls by early man. Before the age of photography, the only way to record an image of a portrait or the full figure was by painting it. You can be part of that history by learning how to paint and draw portraits and the human figure.

For creating realistic and proportionally accurate figures, here are some guidelines to help you understand how to draw both male and female figures. The method to use was first invented by the Renaissance artists and is still the most common method today. Look at stick figures of a man and woman and then at a fully drawn figure, you should be able see how to apply the one to the other.

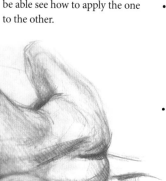

- No two figures are the same, but there are some basic guidelines for you so you can judge the correct proportion.

- Use the head as a unit of measurement, where the 'average' male would be approximately 7.5 heads high. In taller people however, they would be around 8 heads high.

- The torso section of the figure, from the chin to the pubic area, is normally 3 heads tall. You can divide the torso into equal thirds, from the chin to the nipple line, then to the navel, then

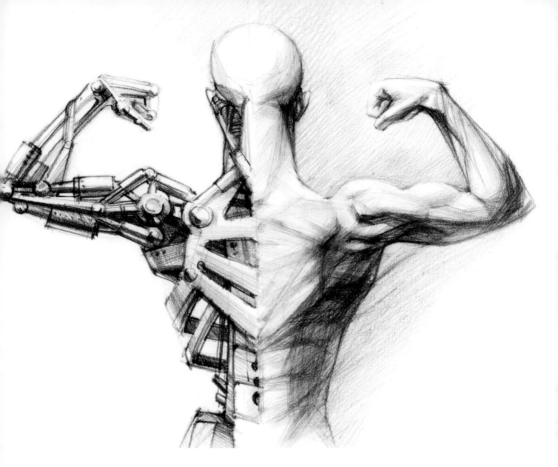

to the pubic area.

- The distance from the upper leg to the knee is approximately 2 heads in length and the lower leg is also the same length.

- The width between the shoulders in a man is around 3 heads wide, whereas a woman's shoulder width is about half a head less.

- From the top of the head to the elbows is roughly 3 heads in length. When standing upright the wrists would be approximately parallel to the pubic area. However, this would change according to the pose of the figure you are drawing.

- The female figure is slightly smaller than the male; a female's hips are usually the same width as her shoulders. This can measure around two heads or a little more.

Proportions of the head

The basic design you can use for a head is one that is oval shaped, with the tapered end at the bottom and the neck can be just a simple cylinder.

This basic shape can now be divided into rough proportions, which will give a stylised version of a human head and features. It is important to remember that every face is different, so you will have to practice and experiment to master the techniques of getting a good likeness.

Portrait and Figure details

To build up your confidence in painting figures or portraits, you should practice making lots of quick sketches of different parts of the body and face.

The human body is affected by different positions, so careful observation is called for, particularly when you draw a figure close up.

Just as in still life or landscape drawing, the body is affected by the rules perspective. One aspect of this is the figure closest to you will seem proportionally larger than a figure further away.

With plenty of practise you will gain your confidence to attempt more complex poses. Start by drawing the subject in to basic simple shapes then you can add the detail, once you are happy with the proportions and position of the features.

WWF is the world's largest nature conservation organization and global environment network. It has nearly 5 million members and is active in about 100 countries. WWF campaigns to protect biodiversity (the variety of life on Earth), to reduce pollution and waste, and to encourage sustainable development. It was originally called the World Wildlife Fund but is now more usually known as WWF to reflect its broader environmental concerns.

WWF's main aims are: to protect and conserve endangered species and address global threats to nature by seeking long-term solutions to the planet's environmental problems.

 Checklist

WWF aims to protect natural habitats and all the species that live in them by:
- raising funds for conservation projects world wide
- creating protected areas
- lobbying governments on environmental issues
- providing scientific expertise
- researching and campaigning to raise levels of environmental awareness

▼ *This panda in the Wolong Nature Reserve in China is protected as part of WWF's Operation Panda.*

 Checklist

1948 The IUCN (see opposite) is set up.

1961 WWF is set up after the Morges Manifesto is signed by world conservation experts.

1986 WWF adopts the name World Wide Fund for Nature, except in the US and Canada where it remains the World Wildlife Fund. In 2001, the global organization becomes known simply as WWF.

1992 The Earth Summit – the world's first global conference on the environment – is held in Rio de Janeiro, Brazil.

2002 WWF launches a campaign to persuade governments to approve the Kyoto Agreement to reduce pollution linked to global warming.

Origins

WWF was formed in 1961 and was the first international organization that set out to save endangered wildlife world wide. Its work began when wildlife experts became worried about the fall in the number of wild animals in western Africa, which could lead to their extinction if not stopped. The naturalist Sir Peter Scott was then Vice President of the IUCN, an organization which researched and collected data on nature conservation. He suggested that a new organization should be set up to raise funds for conservation projects, working in partnership with the IUCN. This became the World Wildlife Fund (WWF). Its first campaigns included projects to save endangered species like the tiger and the rhinoceros.

By 1980, WWF had announced a new World Conservation Strategy. Its policies and campaigns expanded from the protection of species and natural habitats, to include issues such as sustainable farming and energy, global warming and climate change.

▲ *The Northern White Rhino, Zaire – the world's rarest rhino and a seriously endangered species.*

Spotlight

In the late 1950s, hundreds of people visited London Zoo to see the Giant Panda Chi-Chi. At that time, pandas were one of the species that were in danger of becoming extinct, which is why Chi-Chi was chosen as the logo for WWF, designed by Sir Peter Scott.

Spotlight

Tony Cunningham is the Africa Regional Co-ordinator for WWF's People and Plants project. He has helped identify sites that are important habitats for plants and animals and campaigned for alternatives to wild plants that have become endangered. People and Plants works with local people in Africa and other countries to protect the variety of plant life and develop sustainable harvesting of plants.

2. How does WWF work?

WWF has its headquarters in Gland, Switzerland, where its staff, the Secretariat, are based. Around the world, it has a network of organizations that help manage its activities. The national organizations, like WWF-UK, and WWF-US, are all independent, but they work closely together on global projects. Programme offices carry out fieldwork, advise local and national governments and educate local communities on conservation issues.

▼ *Sponsored events raise awareness and funds for WWF campaigns.*

Funding

Almost half of WWF's income comes from its membership fees and another 13 per cent comes from money left in wills or as gifts. The national offices raise funds to run projects in their own countries, and richer ones contribute about two-thirds of their income to global conservation programmes. Volunteers around the world help with fundraising by organizing activities such as sponsored events. WWF also receives income from government grants and aid agencies. WWF raises funds through partnerships with business and industry. Another source of funding is the 1001 Nature Trust. This is made up of 1001 individuals who have given large sums of money to the organization.

● Spotlight

Volunteers play an important part in fundraising for WWF by taking part in sponsored events like bicycle rides, walks and swims. In 1999, over 5000 people in the UK took part in a Great WWF Shark Swim to raise funds for the shark and other endangered marine species. Many species of shark could become extinct because they are hunted for their meat, liver, oil and fins.

Team work

WWF works as an independent, non party-political organization. It runs conservation projects in partnership with governments, international organizations and aid agencies, non-governmental organizations, businesses and local communities.

▲ Local fishermen attend a WWF workshop on sustainable fishing practices in the Banc D'Arguin National Park, Mauritania.

One of WWF's many conservation programmes involved working with the government of Peru and the Peruvian Association for the Protection of Nature (APECO) to protect Manu National Park. WWF provided rangers, jeeps and equipment to protect the park from settlers. The project engaged local people in tree- and crop-planting schemes, helping them to develop sustainable farming methods. WWF recognises that involving local people is vital to the success of any conservation programme. Often, they are facing difficulties such as a shortage of food or water, which have to be overcome first for conservation to succeed.

▲ As part of a conservation programme in Nigeria, local people harvest new crops that have been grown on deforested land.

Co-operation between WWF and local people for the sake of the environment has not only affected rainforest areas and other land habitats, but also benefited the world's oceans. WWF has worked with people from various nations to try and reduce the number of nations fishing international waters for their fish quota. Through its policy of monitoring the number of species in all environments, WWF became aware of the serious decline in numbers of various species of fish used in the food industry. It has warned all nations of the dangers of overfishing in certain waters, and by working in collaboration with the countries involved, has put measures in place to lessen the risk of extinction to endangered marine species.

 ## Spotlight

In the 1970s and 80s, there was so much over-fishing that some stocks, such as the herring fisheries in the North Sea, were almost exhausted. In 1996, WWF worked in partnership with Unilever, the world's largest buyer of frozen fish, to set up the Marine Stewardship Council (MSC). This is a scheme that aims to conserve endangered fish stocks by using the MSC mark to show which fish have come from sustainable fisheries.

 ## Spotlight

WWF's Endangered Seas Campaign has been working with people in the Galapagos Islands and Mauritania to improve marine protected areas. They have created no-take zones and taught native fishermen sustainable fishing methods in order to try and prevent fish stocks from being exhausted.

Imaraguen fishermen from Mauritania fish for golden mullet. WWF has taught them to use nets that do not trap young fish, helping them practise sustainable fishing methods.

3. Species conservation

We share our planet with about 1.8 million known animal and plant species. But scientists believe that we may only have discovered about one-seventh of all the species on Earth. They call the variety of life on Earth biodiversity. WWF has made the protection of biodiversity one of its main aims.

Scientists estimate that about 6,500 animal species and over 30,000 plant species are currently endangered and could become extinct. Many animal species are endangered because of hunting, or illegal poaching. They include tigers, rhinos and elephants. They are hunted for their skins, bones, horns and other animal parts that are used to make clothes, jewellery or traditional types of medicine, which some people believe cure disease. They may also be endangered because their natural habitat is being destroyed for farming or development.

▲ By 2010, there may be no tigers left in the wild if current rates of poaching are allowed to continue.

▶ Elephants increasingly have to compete for their habitat with growing human populations.

Spotlight

WWF is working on a project to protect Indonesia's endangered Javan rhino in the Ujung Kulon National Park. There are between 50 and 60 Javan rhinos remaining in the wild in Indonesia and Vietnam. They live in thick forests but local people were cutting down trees for firewood, destroying their habitat. WWF is helping the people to grow crops like ginger to give them an income, and to plant more trees to supply the wood they need for fuel and cooking.

Biodiversity

We are facing the greatest extinction of animals and plants on Earth since the dinosaurs died out 65 million years ago. Biodiversity is an important part of the natural balance of our planet. WWF aims to protect all species by creating protected wildlife areas and by planting and protecting more forests. WWF works with local communities to protect wildlife and educate people on the importance of biodiversity. It campaigns against the trade in animal parts and funds anti-poaching teams and equipment.

▼ *The Snow Leopard is endangered by hunting for its fur and also by falling numbers of its prey, such as wild sheep and goats.*

Stopping trade in endangered species

There are already controls on wildlife trade through CITES, the Convention on International Trade in Endangered Species. The illegal trade in wildlife is thought to be worth about $20 billion a year. It includes animal furs, ivory, exotic animals for the pet market, plants and fish. In 1976, WWF and the IUCN set up TRAFFIC, a watchdog organization for trade in wildlife. Its staff work through a network of 21 offices, sometimes as under-cover investigators.

▲ *Amazon parrots are caged for export from Argentina as part of the trade in exotic pets.*

● Spotlight

In 1979, WWF set up Operation Panda in the Wolong Nature Reserve, a breeding station and research unit in China. Pandas are endangered because of poaching, the destruction of their natural habitat and a shortage of bamboo, which is their only food. WWF is funding the planting of bamboo corridors so that pandas can move from one protected area to another to find more food.

Problem

In 1971, there were around 65,000 black rhinos in Africa. By the 1990s, just 3000 were left. Trade in rhino horn is illegal, but a poacher can earn enough money from one horn to feed his family for months. When people are faced with problems of poverty, conservation issues may not seem important to them. WWF works with local people to educate them on the importance of conservation and help them find ways of making a living without poaching.

◀ The Giant Panda is at risk because of a shortage of bamboo.

 These illegal supplies of ivory and animal pelts intended for trade on the black market were seized by officials in Tanzania.

● Spotlight

Botanist Reza Azmi is WWF's scientific officer working on a WWF-Malaysia project to preserve the biodiversity of plants in the country. Reza collects specimens of plants which he identifies and catalogues. His studies of plants and their natural habitats will lead to a better understanding of which species are endangered and the major threats to their habitats.

4. Marine conservation

Oceans and seas cover 70 per cent of our planet, but only a tiny fraction are protected areas. In the last 50 years, marine life has come under threat from pollution, over-fishing and coastal development.

WWF's marine policies aim to create a global network of marine protected areas, to promote good coastal management and to reduce and stop marine pollution. They also work to encourage sustainable fishing practices and conserve endangered marine species.

▲ *Sand eel are landed at Esbjerg in Denmark. They are one of many species endangered by over-fishing in the North Sea.*

▲ *Killing with harpoons and dynamite has brought many whale species, including the humpback, close to extinction.*

◖ Problem

The International Whaling Commission (IWC) has failed to stop the hunting of whales. Countries including Japan and Norway have continued to hunt species like the minke whale, claiming that they do so for scientific purposes. Since 1992, the number of whales killed every year has been rising, and the IWC is now facing a crisis as these countries are constantly trying to find new ways of justifying their actions and challenging its powers.

WWF researches and reports on problems that affect marine life. It also campaigns for better controls of trade in marine species through international agreements between countries fishing the same waters, and for changes to fishing equipment. These include the kind of nets that can trap and kill marine creatures such as dolphins, turtles and porpoises.

▲ A patrol boat funded by WWF guards the fisheries in the Banc D'Arguin National Park in Mauretania to prevent illegal fishing by large trawlers.

▲ Coral reefs are rich marine habitats. Many are now endangered by pollution and by changes due to global warming.

Save the whale

By the middle of the last century the use of harpoons and dynamite had destroyed many species of whale, and seven out of eleven species of great whale were close to extinction. In the 1970s, hundreds of people joined anti-whaling rallies and campaigns to Save the Whale yet some countries have continued to hunt them.

▲ *The enormous and powerful tail of a sperm whale – one of the endangered great whale species.*

● Spotlight

Phang-Nga Bay in Thailand is under threat from trawlers and other large fishing vessels that ignore local fishing regulations and fines and are exhausting fish stocks. WWF is working with local communities to help protect the area, which includes mangroves and seagrass habitats. It has funded a team of field workers and is giving practical help in managing the coast and enforcing fishing regulations.

▼ *A mangrove forest in Thailand. More than 50 per cent of these forests have been destroyed for shrimp farming.*

Forests are home to over half of the world's animal and plant species, and scientists believe they may contain hundreds of thousands more species still to be discovered.

Forests help balance our planet's climate. Trees absorb carbon dioxide and pump out oxygen, acting as the planet's lungs. They also recycle rainfall, preventing floods and droughts. But every year, millions of hectares of the world's forests are being destroyed for ever, for timber or firewood or to clear land for farming or development. Scientists estimate that the world has already lost up to two-thirds of its forests, and by 2050 there may be no natural forests left in countries such as Indonesia, Malaysia and Costa Rica.

▼ An aerial view of the Amazon rainforest in Brazil. WWF and the World Bank are working together to protect 25 million hectares of Brazilian forest.

Problem

In 1997, forest fires in Indonesia destroyed vast areas of natural forest and caused a poisonous smog to cover much of the country, killing endangered wildlife including orang utans and rhinos. These fires are believed to have been started illegally by logging companies to clear the land quickly. WWF is lobbying governments in the region to change policies such as giving subsidies for logging and agriculture that encourage the burning of forests. WWF is also campaigning for an International Court of the Environment to be set up which could help prevent illegal logging and fire raising.

▼ *Forest fires like this one in Brazil create pollution, erode the soil and ruin the local ecology. Some fires are thought to have been set on purpose to clear land for cattle ranches.*

▲ *A meeting in Indonesia to co-ordinate emergency action to try and stop the increasing number of forest fires.*

WWF has campaigned to save the world's tropical rainforests since 1975. Today, its Forests for Life programme supports over 300 projects in more than 65 countries. It aims to set up a network of protected areas (just 6 per cent of the world's forests are currently protected) and to encourage good forest management outside protected areas. It is also working to develop programmes to restore forests and to reduce forest damage from climate change and pollution.

Spotlight

The forests of the Northern Andes in South America are home to over 200 bird species and 86 species of palm tree, including the world's tallest palm, the wax palm. The area is threatened by farming, ranching, logging and mining, and at least 55 per cent of its forests have been lost. WWF has sent a team of experts to the area. They have drawn up maps showing areas of forest, patterns of land use and population, and are developing a conservation plan to protect the remaining forest.

▼ *Logging in the forest of Riau in Sumatra, Indonesia.*

The Forest Stewardship Council

In 1993, WWF joined other conservation groups and timber companies to form the Forest Stewardship Council. The FSC sets standards for sustainable forest management. Companies agree to buy and sell only from well-managed forests, and the public can choose to buy timber products with the FSC trademark.

> ▶ *A harvest of bamboo is transported by raft down a river in Sulawesi, Indonesia.*

 Spotlight

In Quintana Roo, Mexico, WWF is helping local Mayan peoples to manage 150,000 hectares of forest in sustainable ways. They run their own saw mills and sell forest products including timber, pepper and honey through a workers' co-operative. This means that the local people have an income from the forest and have an interest in protecting it.

6. Freshwater and wetland conservation

Wetlands cover just 6 per cent of the Earth's surface but they are vital to the natural balance of our planet. They include mangrove swamps, marshes, estuaries, tidal flats and shallow seas. Wetlands add to and purify the Earth's water reserves and help protect coastal areas. They are also important wildlife habitats.

Many of the world's wetlands are under threat. They are being damaged by rising sea levels due to global warming and by pollution from chemicals like pesticides being washed into rivers. Others are lost because of land drainage for farming or river engineering schemes. Some countries have already lost between 50 to 80 per cent of their wetlands.

▲ An aerial view of the Rapadalen Delta in Sweden. Deltas, where rivers meet the sea, provide a fertile wetland habitat.

◖ Problem

Dams and embankments can help provide water and energy for a growing population, but they can also endanger or destroy precious wetlands. In Iceland, there are plans to flood up to 180 square kilometres of wilderness in Snaefell. Reservoirs will be linked by tunnels to a power station, which will power the production of aluminium. WWF is campaigning to protect the area as a national park because it provides a natural habitat for around 3000 reindeer, 310 plant species and dozens of species of birds. In 2003 the Icelandic parliament backed the reservoir project, despite a report that said it would damage the environment. WWF and other organizations have promised to continue fighting the project, and have urged the Icelandic government to find another source of energy for the aluminium plant.

In 1971, over 100 countries signed the Ramsar Convention which pledged to protect threatened wetlands. Over 1000 valuable wetland sites are now protected. WWF launched its Wetlands Conservation Fund in 1990, to fund projects to conserve wetlands under threat in developing countries. WWF experts advise local governments, prepare wetland conservation and management plans and train people to become wetland rangers. WWF is building databases of wetland sites.

▼ *A peat bog in the Vosges mountains in France. Peat bogs are ancient wildlife habitats.*

The water crisis

Water covers two-thirds of our planet's surface but only 2.5 per cent of that is freshwater. Most of it is found as groundwater or in the polar ice-caps and glaciers, leaving only a tiny fraction available in lakes and rivers. About 1.3 billion people in the world today don't have access to safe drinking water, and United Nations experts predict that by 2025, two-thirds of the world's population could face serious water shortages. The water crisis is caused by natural factors such as drought but also by pollution and poor water management.

WWF's Freshwater Programme, and the Endangered Seas Campaign, launched in 1999, aim to protect freshwater reserves for people and the environment.

▲ A beach in Venezuela, polluted by rubbish left by tourists.

▼ The North Sea is polluted by the dumping of sewage and other waste matter.

7. Climate change

In the 1970s, scientists began to report changes in the Earth's climate. They detected a 'greenhouse effect', which was warming up the Earth's temperature. Waste gases from cars and industry, including carbon dioxide, were trapping heat from the sun in the Earth's atmosphere, leading to global warming.

▲ *Parched earth in Thailand shows the effects of severe drought.*

They also began to detect holes in the ozone layer which protects the planet from the sun's dangerous rays. These were being caused by the effect of chemicals polluting the Earth's atmosphere. Records show that the tropics are getting hotter and drier, and the Sahara Desert is expanding. The Antarctic and Arctic ice sheets are breaking up and as a result, sea levels are an average 20 centimetres higher world wide than they were 100 years ago. Around 80 per cent of the world's beaches are now being worn away by rising sea levels.

Some scientists predict that sea levels will rise by up to half a metre by the end of this century, if the greenhouse effect goes on increasing. Most scientists now agree that global warming could have disastrous effects on the human population and the environment. There will be more extremes of weather, such as droughts, floods, storms and hurricanes. Diseases such as malaria could spread in a warmer climate to affect up to a third of the world's population.

▼ *Violent weather effects such as tornadoes are becoming more frequent due to global warming.*

 Spotlight

WWF–Netherlands worked with five of the largest building firms in the country on a scheme to build 200 energy-efficient homes. It is also working with Swiss and American technology firms to develop solar power for heating and lighting.

▲ *Rising sea levels are leading to devastating floods in low-lying countries like Bangladesh.*

 Spotlight

In Poland, the country's poor energy efficiency meant that for every hour of electricity used, three times more carbon dioxide was being produced than in Germany. WWF has been funding projects to make Polish people aware of the hazards of wasting energy. Schools and businesses have been sent information packs on how to save energy in the home, such as using low-energy light bulbs.

The Climate Change Campaign

WWF launched its Climate Change Campaign in the 1990s. The main goal of the campaign is to protect the environment by reducing levels of greenhouse gases in the atmosphere. WWF is lobbying governments to take steps to achieve this. Measures include switching from fossil fuels (oil, coal, gas) to clean, sustainable sources of energy such as wind, wave and solar power, cutting energy waste, investing in public transport to reduce the number of cars on the roads, and making industry pay a climate-change tax.

Forest preservation and climate change

Another way to reduce global warming is to stop the destruction of forests, which absorb carbon dioxide from the Earth's atmosphere. Scientists believe that the loss of forests could add up to 10 billion tonnes of carbon dioxide to the Earth's atmosphere every year.

 Spotlight

WWF has funded a tree-planting programme in Virunga National Park, on the border of Zaire Rwanda in Africa.

▲ *Forest workers in Brazil take mahogany tree seedlings to be planted in areas of rainforest that have been damaged. It takes twenty five years for mahogany trees to reach maturity.*

Since WWF was founded, the human population has almost doubled to more than 6 billion people. Every year, more forest, farmland and wildlife habitats are lost to development. Pollution has increased and is leading to changes in the global climate. Water reserves are falling and areas of desert increasing. Experts believe that the human population will more than double again by the middle of the twenty-first century, putting more of a strain on the Earth's natural resources.

▲ In the Americas and Europe, about seven in ten people live in cities. Cities such as La Paz in Bolivia, shown here, are among the most densely populated areas of the world.

Problem

By 2000, half the world's population was living in cities. Cities take up just 2 per cent of the Earth's land surface, but use 75 per cent of its resources. In future, just supplying enough fresh water to the world's growing cities could be a major challenge. WWF has produced a report making recommendations for new measures, such as planting more forests, rainwater harvesting, and educating local communities on water management and conservation.

WWF estimates that over 30 per cent of the natural world has been destroyed since 1970. But now there are signs that we are becoming more aware of the problems facing the environment.

In 1992, 160 countries and conservation groups met for the Earth Summit. The world's nations agreed to try and reduce global warming, and protect biodiversity. In 1997, some governments signed the Kyoto Agreement, to limit the pollution each country produces and so stop global warming. In 2004, a few leading nations had still not approved the agreement. WWF campaigned for these nations to play their part.

▲ The Tree of Life sculpture at the United Nations Earth Summit held in Rio, Brazil in 1992. WWF was one of many conservation organizations that attended the summit.

Future problems

WWF and other conservation groups face major challenges in the twenty-first century. They include a growing human population and an increasing gap between rich and poor countries. As pollution increases, and natural resources and fossil fuels run out, there could also be disastrous changes in climate due to rising sea levels.

WWF and the future

Without WWF, many species, including tigers, rhinos, polar bears and whales might already have become extinct, and the world would have lost even more of its precious resources like tropical rainforests and wetland habitats. But as the Earth enters a new millennium, nature conservation has never been a greater challenge than it is now.

▲ *Polar bears in the Arctic are one of many species threatened by the effects of global warming.*

▼ *Warmer temperatures are breaking up ice sheets and glaciers, leading to rising sea levels.*

Spotlight

Antarctica has been described as the Earth's last wilderness. As well as being an important wildlife habitat, it helps scientists measure changes in the environment. But in the 1980s, Antarctica came under threat from countries wanting to mine for precious minerals including oil, gold and silver. A conservation plan to save Antarctica was launched and in 1991, an international agreement was reached to protect it from oil and mineral exploration for at least half a century.

biodiversity   the variety of life on Earth

commercial   carried out on a big scale for profit

deforestation   cutting down forests

endangered   in danger of becoming extinct

extinct   died out completely, as in a species

fossil fuels   natural fuels such as coal, oil and gas that are the fossilized remains of long-dead living things

global warming   the increase in the Earth's temperature due to the effect of pollution in the atmosphere

greenhouse effect   the term scientists use to describe gases that trap heat in the Earth's atmosphere, leading to global warming

habitat   the natural environment of a plant, animal, or person

intensive farming   farming methods designed to produce the maximum amount of yield from a piece of land

nature conservation   protecting and managing the Earth and its environment and natural resources

ozone layer   a layer of gas in the Earth's upper atmosphere that protects it from the sun's harmful rays

pesticides   chemicals used to kill insects or other pests that can cause extensive damage to crops. Used widely in intensive farming

subsidies   grants paid by governments

sustainable   describing a method that does not damage the environment or exhaust natural resources

Useful information

WWF International
Avenue du Mont-Blanc
1196 Gland
Switzerland
www.panda.org

WWF-Australia
Level 13
235 Jones Street
Ultimo NSW 2007
www.wwf.org.au

WWF-UK
Panda House
Weyside Park
Godalming
Surrey GU7 1XR
www.wwf.org.uk

WWF-USA
1250 24th Street NW
Washington DC
20037-1175
www.worldwildlife.org

Become a campaigner for conservation:
If you have access to the Internet look up
the website for online campaigners and apply
for a WWF panda passport at
www.passport.panda.org
or find out more about these organizations:

WSPA
Join the Rangers at WSPA (World Society for
the Protection of Animals)
Dept 1R1
Freepost
Melksham SN12 6GZ
www.wspa.org.uk

Greenpeace UK,
Canonbury Villas,
London N1 2PN
www.greenpeace.org

Friends of the Earth,
26–28 Underwood Street,
London N1 7JQ
www.foe.co.uk

Index